POETRY AND THE
PSYCHOLOGY OF COMPASSION

PROFESSOR PATRICK PIETRONI

FRESCO BOOKS

CONTENTS

5   *Feel, Thoink and Act*
Patrick Pietroni

7 INTRODUCTION

   13 *All Rivers at Once*
   Jalal ad-Din Muhammad Rumi

   15 *All the World's a Stage*
   William Shakespeare

12 MODELS OF THE MIND

   17 Psychoanalysts

     18 *Dreams*
     Amitav Radiance

     21 *The Shrink Series 2*
     MS Lim

   24 Behavioural Psychologists

   26 Humanistic Psychologists

     27 *Hierarchy of Needs*
     Maslow

   28 Psychiatrists

   31 Neuroscience, Neuroimaging
   and Neurotransmitters

33 LANGUAGE OF COMPASSION

    36 Intelligent Kindness

    38 Feelings, Thoughts and Actions

39 CULTIVATING COMPASSION

    39 Self Compassion

        41 *Compassion and the Other*
            Patrick Pietroni

    42 Within Educational Establishments

    45 Within Health Care Settings

    48 Global Compassion

FEEL, THINK AND ACT

So easy to say
So difficult to do.
I pass the homeless
On the road every day.
No Samaritan am I
"Feelings" – Oh yes!
Anger
Guilt
Shame
Thoughts – Oh yes!
"Blame them"
"The poor will always
be with us"
"The Council should do
something."
Action – Oh yes!
Press the accelerator
Turn on the radio
Write a poem!
Thank goodness for Scarlett O'Hara
"After all, tomorrow is another day!"

Patrick Pietroni [1]

INTRODUCTION

In the first volume of this series, *The Poetry of Compassion*, I introduced the concept of compassion and how Charles Darwin's research suggests that the human species has evolved to behave compassionately, or at least, that we have the capacity to do so. In the *Descent of Man*, he wrote:

> *"We are ... impelled to relieve the sufferings of another, in order that our own painful feelings may be at the same time relieved. In like manner we are led to participate in the pleasures of others."* [2]

Recent discoveries in neuroscience and neuro-imaging support this biological basis for compassion, but it was Darwin who originally argued that,

> *"[T]hose communities which contained the greatest number of the most sympathetic members would flourish best, and rear the greatest number of offspring"*. [3]

I then outlined using selected poems how the following concepts of compassion could be understood:

Proximal compassion
Distal compassion
Global compassion
Self-compassion
Compassion fatigue

In the second volume, *Poetry and the Science of Compassion*, again using selected poems, I outlined how science, especially how neuroscience has allowed us to understand the biological, chemical, and physical basis of the nature of compassion.

I described how each of the following chemicals (neurotransmitters) has both a specific and general effect on our physical, emotional, and cognitive experience in relation to compassion:

   dopamine, serotonin, endorphin, oxytocin, and cortisol

In the third volume, *The Poetry of Global Compassion*, using Ronald Higgin's approach, again with selected poems, I summarised the seven enemies he outlined in his book (*The Seventh Enemy*[4]). These include:

1. World population growth
2. Food shortage and food facts
3. Alarming environmental degradation
4. Depletion of earth's natural resources
5. The nuclear threat
6. Science and technology galloping at a speed beyond human control
7. The human factor

I ended this third volume by quoting a thirteenth-century Persian poet – Rumi

ALL RIVERS AT ONCE
(extract)

What is the body? Endurance.
What is love? Gratitude.
What is hidden in our chests? Laughter.
What else? Compassion.

Jalal ad-Din Muhammad Rumi [5]

In the fourth volume, The Education for Compassion, I tackle the challenges posed by the question, can we create an educational system that can include a compassionate curriculum? What does such a curriculum include and how should it be delivered?

I chose to explore in greater detail how the compassionate development of a child can be encouraged or not, as he/she journeys through their "three score years and ten" – this must now be changed to "four score years and ten" as many of us live past our 90s.

The poem I chose was by Shakespeare.

ALL THE WORLD'S A STAGE

All the world's a stage,
And all the men and women merely players;
They have their exits and their entrances;
And one man in his time plays many parts,
His acts being seven ages. At first the infant,
Mewling and puking in the nurse's arms;
And then the whining school-boy, with his satchel
And shining morning face, creeping like snail
Unwillingly to school. And then the lover,
Sighing like furnace, with a woeful ballad
Made to his mistress' eyebrow. Then a soldier,
Full of strange oaths, and bearded like the pard,
Jealous in honour, sudden and quick in quarrel,
Seeking the bubble reputation
Even in the cannon's mouth. And then the justice,
In fair round belly with good capon lin'd,
With eyes severe and beard of formal cut,
Full of wise saws and modern instances;
And so he plays his part. The sixth age shifts
Into the lean and slipper'd pantaloon,
With spectacles on nose and pouch on side;
His youthful hose, well sav'd, a world too wide
For his shrunk shank; and his big manly voice,
Turning again toward childish treble, pipes
And whistles in his sound. Last scene of all,
That ends this strange eventful history,
Is second childishness and mere oblivion;
Sans teeth, sans eyes, sans taste, sans everything.

William Shakespeare [6]

In this fifth volume I will outline how the more modern study of the brain using MRI scanning and neural-imagining has enhanced our understanding of the psychology of compassion. I start with a historical review of how our predecessors described the relationship between the brain, the mind, consciousness and emotions.

MODELS OF THE MIND

We take it for granted that our mind is in some way linked with our brain, and if it resides anywhere it must be somewhere in our head. In fact, this is a relatively recent notion, for the Egyptians believed that mind-spirit-soul resided not in the brain but in the bowels and heart. The Sumerians thought it resided in the liver and even the great philosopher Aristotle saw the heart as the seat of thought and feeling. Aristotle, and Plato, his teacher, were the major Western philosophers whose opinions concerning the mind held sway right from 300 BC until the sixteenth and seventeenth centuries. Even now, the study of the mind is hampered by the descriptions outlined thousands of years ago by these two great men. Their observations were a great step forward, but because of their greatness, few individuals had the courage to build on their descriptions. The relationship between

Plato and Aristotle is beautifully expressed in Raphael's majestic fresco "The School of Athens". There we see Plato, with hand upraised pointing to the stars, whereas Aristotle, holding a copy of Plato's book Timaeus, is pointing to the earth. Although Plato is seen as a great rationalist, he did not believe in trusting the senses and arrived at his great description of the mind, knowledge and civilization through a mixture of mystical contemplation and mathematics. Plato's *Republic* gives a description as to how he saw the perfect civilization. The outline is based on an oligarchy (government by the few) and Plato's ideas are relatively hierarchical. Because he valued reason above all other attributes, it followed that it should reside in the topmost part of the body – the head. Plato felt knowledge was better acquired not from observation, but through "vision of truth", and the parable of "the cave" is his clearest description of how man is entrapped and chained by his limited visions.

Aristotle was far more of a realist than Plato and was himself a great biologist. It is ironic that he felt the heart to be the seat of life, the soul and the mind, and that the brain function was the blood that carried the life-force through the body. However, although Aristotle's observations were inaccurate, they were balanced by his foundation of the system of deductive logic which still governs the principles of rational debate to this day. Both Plato and Aristotle were instrumental in seeing the mind's chief faculty as reason and logic, and the early Christian church incorporated some aspects of their philosophies. The early church had a major influence in maintaining the notion that mind, spirit and soul were all closely linked, and to some extent this gave church leaders a certain control over not only the study of the mind but also what the mind should think, feel and imagine. The persecution of the witches and the tortures of the Inquisition were justified because the victims of these activities showed obvious signs of deranged minds. Even though Hippocrates in the fifth century BCE had suggested that epilepsy was a physical disorder, nevertheless many sufferers were subjected to purges, incantations and sacrifices and were seen to be possessed by the Devil. For the church, a healthy mind meant believing in its dogma and an unhealthy mind meant allying oneself with the forces of evil.

It took another two great men to free man from the grip of the church. Leonardo Da Vinci, who insisted on studying the body through dissection and not simply through inference and intuition, described the brain with its hemispheres and ventricles and laid the foundation for modern neuroanatomy. Descartes brought together the principles which established the importance of the mind, separate from the body and the soul. Newton provided the basis for the scientific method by highlighting the power of ration-or-reason, as Aristotle had done earlier. As the result of their studies, the *dualistic* (separating mind from matter-body), the *mechanistic* (regarding the body, including the brain, as a machine) and the *reductionistic* (reducing things to their smallest components) modes of thought and behaviour became the prevalent model that has held sway right up until modern times.

From the seventeenth century onwards, the study of the mind was in some way overshadowed by the study of the body. It was not until the late nineteenth and early twentieth century that further steps were taken to understanding the workings of the mind.

Psychoanalysts, Psychologists, Psychiatrists

Psychoanalysts	Followers of Freud, may or may not be medical doctors
Psychologists	Study workings of the mind, not medical doctors
Psychiatrists	Medical doctors treating mental disorders, usually with drugs
Psychotherapists	Medical doctors or non-medical doctors who treat mental disorders without drugs.

Psychoanalysts

Sigmund Freud stands out as one of the great innovators in the study of the mind. He studied medicine and neurology and was initially influenced by Breuer, who used hypnosis to release painful memories in cases of hysteria. Many of the patients Freud saw in Vienna were heavily influenced by the social prohibitions on sexual matters. It appeared to Freud that the painful memories released, first through hypnosis and then through "free association", invariably contained a sexual content.

DREAMS

As I go to sleep
Dreams come knocking
My subconscious mind
In a rendezvous with me
Am I asleep?
The REM phase kicks in
What do I want to view?
I do not have a choice
I am just a spectator
For another movie
Do I know the cast or crew?
Is it a blockbuster or horror movie?
The conclusion is inconclusive
I may not be a protagonist
Maybe a figment of my imagination
Or, a vivid description of my days events
It requires psychoanalysis
My subconscious mind is in control
Why can't I have control?
It's not within my control
I am asleep and my mind is awake
Freud wrote extensively about it -
In the 'Interpretation of Dreams'
But still, outside our realm of understanding
The symbols and motifs can give clue
Ancient cultures have recorded on clay tablets
But we may not be ever sure
Or maybe the soul is guided somewhere
Or it could be our inner desires

Maybe it's an unknown world
Where we go out to venture
Let there be beautiful dreams
And dreams that inspire
Or, a vivid description of my days events
It requires psychoanalysis
My subconscious mind is in control
Why can't I have control?
It's not within my control
I am asleep and my mind is awake
Freud wrote extensively about it-
In the 'Interpretation of Dreams'
But still, outside our realm of understanding
The symbols and motifs can give clue
Ancient cultures have recorded on clay tablets
But we may not be ever sure
Or maybe the soul is guided somewhere
Or it could be our inner desires
Maybe it's an unknown world
Where we go out to venture
Let there be beautiful dreams
And dreams that inspire

Amitav Radiance [7]

Freud reintroduced the concept of "energy" into the workings of the mind and labelled this energy "libido". He went on to describe two models of the mind which still form the basis of much psychoanalytic thinking. The first divided the mind into *conscious, preconscious* and *unconscious*. The conscious part of the mind contains all immediately accessible information and memories of present and past experiences. The preconscious contains those memories that, with an effort of will, we can recall, and the unconscious is the repository of all that is forgotten or repressed, and, Freud felt, other painful events. Psychoanalysis is the process by which we can make the unconscious material available to our conscious mind. Freud thought that as long as important events remained unconscious, the mind would remai limited in its capabilities and primate in its behaviour. The second model of the mind included the *ego* (conscious part, aware of the self), the *super-ego* (judging critical part influenced by parents, teachers, priests) and the *id* (unconscious, childlike, primitive part). Freud saw psychoanalysis as a means of strengthening the ego and releasing it from the influences of the super-ego and id i.e. we have a *higher self* that tells, guides, judges, criticises, leads and directs us; a *middle self* which is the way we operate on an everyday practical basis, and a *lower self* which contains our instincts, drives, uncontrolled urges and habit patterns.

The study of the mind therefore was the study of how "Colonel Super-ego", "Lieutenant Ego" and "Private Id" got on together. Freud called the language used by the ego and super-ego "secondary process" and that used by id "primary process", which included the language of dreams, slips of the tongue, free association. Freud felt that the balance between super-ego, ego and id was heavily influenced by the early experiences provided by the parents and that the mind was shaped and moulded by the relationships between father, mother and infant.

THE SHRINK SERIES 2
(extract)

1
Sigmund Freud's sexuality theory -
not everyone could agree with or applaud
some critics wrote derisively:
'His name should have been spelt Sickman Fraud'

MS Lim [8]

Many of Freud's followers have since altered and added to his theories, but his fundamental descriptions of the unconscious elements in the mind still stand as his major achievement and retain their influence to this day. Jung, initially Freud's closest follower, described a very separate area in the workings of the mind. He felt that not only did the mind have a *personal unconscious* as a result of the individual's early experiences, but that the mind was also influenced by collective unconscious. By that he meant that the mind had access to and was influenced by all the collective memories of the race, culture, society, nation to which that individual belonged. Freud dismissed this idea as fanciful and unscientific, but again, like Freud's own discoveries, it links well with several older descriptions of the mind.

Thank God I am Jung and not a Jungian – Carl Jung [9]

The fascination that we have for myths, legend, folklore, fairy stories, parables and rituals indicates the links between the personal mind and the collective mind. Jung studied these collective experiences and described in detail how he felt the individual mind was shaped by them. He compared these collective experiences in different cultures and was able to identify recurring themes, such as the hero myth (Ulysses, Robin Hood).

Between them, Freud and Jung discovered, like the voyagers of old, new territories in the mind — Personal and Collective Unconscious.

Behavioural Psychologists

A totally different line of enquiry was followed by the early psychologists who treated the mind as if it were a physical entity, linked entirely to the workings of the brain. This group of psychologists were known as *behavioural psychologists* because they felt the appropriate way to study the mind was to study how it affected the behaviour of the individual. They applied the scientific measuring instruments used in other disciplines to help determine how the mind functioned. They saw the mind as being influenced by "conditioning". The mind responded to a stimulus (food), by a response (eating). The response was either rewarded (hunger assuaged) or punished (feeling sick). Skinner, the most eminent of this group, believed that all behaviour could be explained by the various permutation and combinations of this simple sequence.

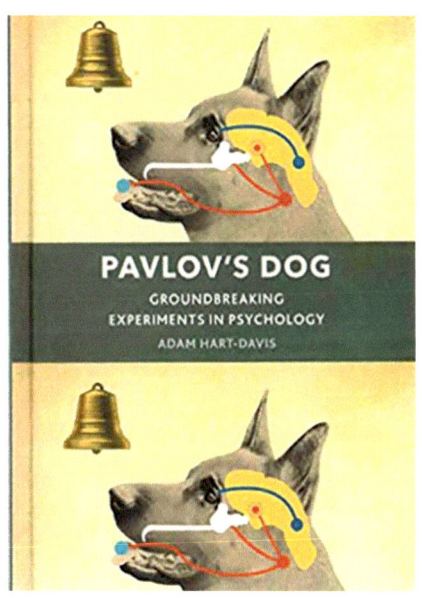

The classical experiments by Pavlov illustrated this scientifically; Pavlov rang bells and gave dogs food at the same time. He found that after a while, he would ring the bells and the dogs would salivate even though no food was present.

For Skinner, all phenomena of the mind could be explained through the science of behaviourism, and in the most extreme form of this theory he maintained that "free will" was an illusion described by idealists who refused to accept the proofs of his discoveries. Behavioural psychology has led to treating mental disturbances as if they were inappropriate conditioned responses. If you are afraid of flying, the mental response to entering an airplane has nothing to do with your past early experience or, if they do, it is irrelevant to subsequent treatment. The individual with a fear is gradually introduced to the stimulus (airplane) and is rewarded every time he is able to reduce his fear or punished if his response is "wrong". Behavioural psychologists introduced a new and important dimension to the study of the mind which appeared to be in total opposition to that of the analysts, and certainly their methods of treating mental disorders were very different.

Humanistic Psychologists

The next group of psychologists who studied the mind were the *humanistic psychologists*. This group felt that it was unhelpful to reduce the mind to the Freudian mental structure of super-ego, ego and id, or the experimental processes of operant conditioning described by Skinner and his followers. They felt these "models" somehow did not describe the essential experience of being human. They looked to existential philosophers for their inspiration. Maslow, a major writer in this area, outlined the need the mind has for reaching its full potential through creative acts.

Humanistic psychologists studied the workings of the mind by studying especially creative or gifted people. They emphasised the healthy aspects of the mind and laid the foundation to the "positive thinking" school. Think positively and you will behave positively. They emphasised the strength of the conscious mind and its ability to overcome the *unconscious* influences. Therapists trained in this model of the mind limit the exploration of "unconscious tendencies" and do not expose their clients to controlled behaviour modifications. They tend to focus on the enhancement of the individual's emotional life and reinforce the positive and healthy tendencies already present. They focus on the "here and now" rather than the past or future.

MASLOW'S HIERARCHY OF NEEDS

I've recently perused the work of *Maslow*,
who's well-known for his quite perceptive claims:
he says the needs that every person has go
from basic ones like food to higher aims.
The *Physiological* needs come first - survival
requires us to eat, to drink, to sleep.
When those are met, then *Safety* starts to rival
them for attention, since we have a deep
desire to be protected. Then comes *Love*
and Belonging: we need family and friends
to stave off loneliness. And then above
this stage, there's self-Esteem. Our health depends
on these four all being met, so motivation
impels us to *Self-actualisation*.

Discoveria [10]

Psychiatrists

Psychiatrists who use drugs or ECT (electroconvulsive therapy, which is electrical stimulation of the brain) to manage mental disorders see the mind like the behaviourists, as a function of the brain. The brain is like other organs in the body and can be studied using the instruments that doctors have used to study other organs. They have been influenced therefore by the neuroanatomists and neurophysiologists who have studied the brain and the mind with increasing success in the last twenty to thirty years.

For centuries, men have drilled holes in the skull, probed and explored the brain using surgical and, more recently, electrical instruments. In the last thirty years brain surgeons have severed connections in the brain in an attempt to cure epilepsy and portions of the brain have been removed to treat personality disorders.

In more recent years, the electroencephalograph (EEG) has been used to measure electrical activity arising from the brain and, as with a jigsaw puzzle, the link between the anatomical parts of the brain and its functions is slowly being discovered. For the purposes of this book we shall limit ourselves to a description of the mental functions of the brain and the way they influence our daily life. The major part of the brain is made up of two hemispheres joined by millions of neurons (nerve cells with long connecting threads). The left hemisphere controls the movement on the right side of the body and the right hemisphere controls the left side of the body. In addition, the left hemisphere governs those functions principally to do with speech, rational thought, logical reasoning, objective analysis, whilst

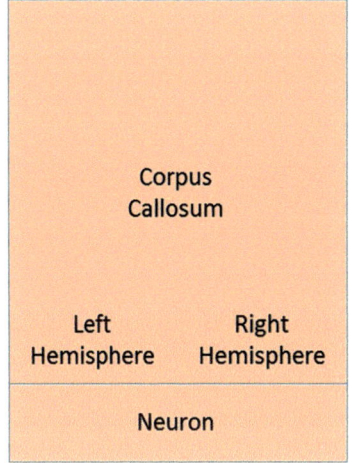

	Left *Hemisphere*	Right *Hemisphere*
Corpus Callosum	Thoughts Linear reason Verbal Objective Mathematics Literature	Feeling Initiative Non-verbal Subjective Images Patterns/ Shape
Left Hemisphere Right Hemisphere Neuron	Extrovert Reading Analysis	Introvert Rhythm Synthesis

the right hemisphere is concerned with how things relate to one another.

The right hemisphere recognises shapes, patterns and images, and it covers our intuitive sense. It appears that each hemisphere can function independently of the other, but that in most people one hemisphere plays a more dominant role. For most people the left hemisphere is the dominant hemisphere, resulting in more right-handed people. Not only does the dominant hemisphere govern the movement and handedness but it seems to determine the pre-vailing "consciousness" or mode of thought.

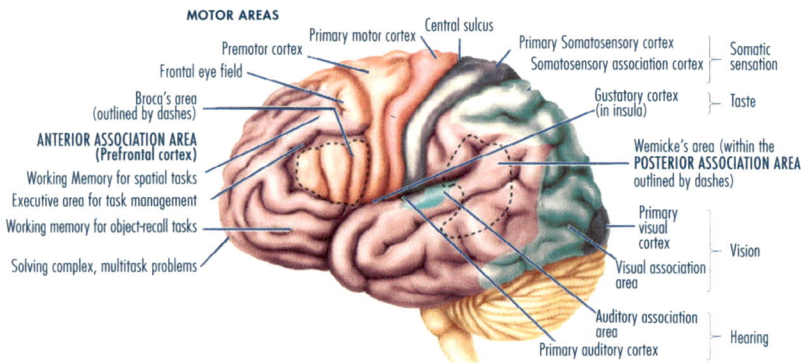

SENSORY AREAS & RELATED ASSOCIATION AREAS

MOTOR AREAS

Central sulcus

Primary motor cortex

Premotor cortex

Frontal eye field

Broca's area
(outlined by dashes)

ANTERIOR ASSOCIATION AREA
(Prefrontal cortex)

Working Memory for spatial tasks

Executive area for task management

Working memory for object-recall tasks

Solving complex, multitask problems

Primary Somatosensory cortex — Somatic
Somatosensory association cortex — sensation

Gustatory cortex — Taste
(in insula)

Wernicke's area (within the
POSTERIOR ASSOCIATION AREA
outlined by dashes)

Primary
visual — Vision
cortex

Visual association
area

Auditory association
area — Hearing

Primary auditory cortex

LEFT CEREBRAL HEMISPHERE – LATERAL VIEW

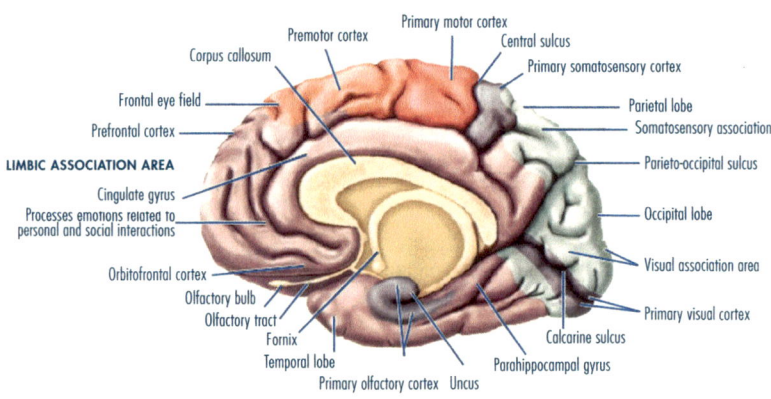

Premotor cortex

Primary motor cortex

Corpus callosum

Central sulcus

Primary somatosensory cortex

Frontal eye field

Prefrontal cortex

Parietal lobe

Somatosensory association

LIMBIC ASSOCIATION AREA

Cingulate gyrus

Processes emotions related to
personal and social interactions

Parieto-occipital sulcus

Occipital lobe

Orbitofrontal cortex

Olfactory bulb

Olfactory tract

Fornix

Temporal lobe

Primary olfactory cortex   Uncus

Visual association area

Primary visual cortex

Calcarine sulcus

Parahippocampal gyrus

RIGHT HEMISPHERE – PARASAGITTAL VIEW

- Primary motor cortex
- Motor association cortex
- Primary sensory cortex
- Sensory association cortex
- Multimodal association cortex

Neuroscience, Neuroimaging and Neurotransmitters

There has been an enormous advance in the understanding of brain structures and brain functioning with the development of brain imagining techniques. This has allowed researchers and brain surgeons to pinpoint both anatomical disorders e.g. brain tumours, as well as the location of how the brain functions. Magnetic Resonance Imaging (MRI) allows us to be more precise as to which part of the brain "lights up" when we perform separate tasks such as reading, sleeping, dreaming – or when we experience emotions such as anger, compassion, memory recall etc. These mapping techniques are still in their infancy and caution needs to be applied that sometimes is not heeded in the articles found in more popular journals. Most brain researchers agree that there is a degree of "plasticity" in the functions of different parts of the brain. Another model, the "triune brain", was first described by Paul MacLean. Carl Sagan in his groundbreaking book, The *Dragons of Eden* [11], was responsible for making this model popular. However, this is no longer considered to be as definite as first described. It does provide a helpful description of the evolution of the mammalian brain. The model suggests the following:

Reptilian brain   Governs our basic instinct
Limbic system   Governs our emotional and expressive
                 behaviour
Frontal cortex   Governs our thoughts, language, judgement

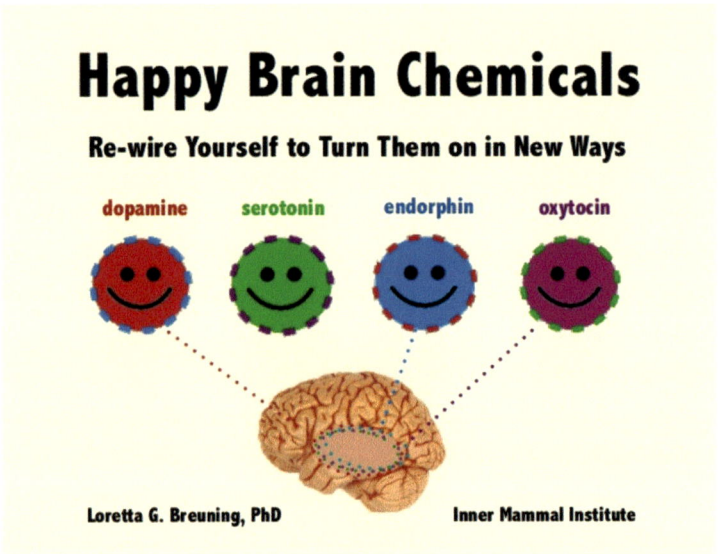

Neurotransmitters

In my second book in this series, *Poetry and the Science of Compassion,* I describe how chemical substances act as "neuro-modulators" i.e. they facilitate the transfer of electrical activity between one neuron and another. Loretta Breuning [12] has produced an excellent slide show on these modulators which she labels as the "Happy Brain Chemicals". They include oxytocin; serotonin; endorphin; dopamine; cortisol.

THE LANGUAGE OF COMPASSION

Many of the words used by researchers, academics and therapists involved in the study of compassion seem to multiply exponentially with each journal publication. At my last count there are between 100-150 words and phrases that the different disciplines use (and indeed argue over). I am sure someone somewhere is putting together a Dictionary of Compassion. I have chosen to limit myself to no more than twelve words and illustrate them with a little story.

What's What in the Compassion Tool Box

Compassion and the Exhausted Marathon Runner

You are in a pub/bar on a hot summer day and are about to order a drink. You hear the pub door swing open and a man staggers in drenched in sweat. He is dressed indicating he has just run a marathon. He looks at you and says, "Sorry, I have no money":

Sympathy	is if you say, "Don't worry, I will buy you one"
Empathy	is when you see his sweaty face, you say, "You are making me feel thirsty as well. I will buy myself the same drink"
Compassion	is after you both have finished your drinks you say, "My car is outside, can I give you a lift somewhere?"
Kindness	is not minding when he vomits all over your car because you bought him a very cold pint of light beer when he had asked for some warm lemonade
Concern	is when he passes out in your car and urinates
Intelligent Kindness	is when you decide to take him to the nearest hospital
Relief	is when you arrive home and vow to not take pity on anyone again
Altruism	is what you believe your behaviour to have been

Irritation	is when your wife tells you off for sitting on the sofa with vomit all over your clothes
Anger	is what you feel when she tells you are always trying to play the Good Samaritan and that charity should begin at home
Insight	is when deep down you know she is right and that you have all too often refused to mow the lawn when she asks you to, or do the washing up
Reflection	is when you decide you will go and see a counsellor, start jogging, and you arrive at your first session having run from your home
Your Breakdown	is when the counsellor notices you are sweating and asks whether you want a drink.

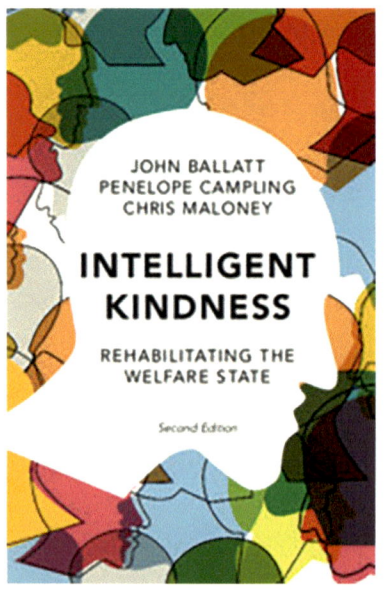

Intelligent Kindness

Clearly, it would take a very large book to explore and describe how psychologists, sociologists, anthropologists and evolutionists understand and study the concept of compassion. I have chosen to elaborate on one of these books: *Intelligent Kindness: Reforming the Culture of Healthcare* [13] is written by two of my close colleagues, John Ballatt and Penelope Campling. They have both worked in the National Health Service and Social Care for many years. A second edition has just been published: *Intelligent Kindness: Rehabilitating the Welfare State* co-written by Ballatt, Campling and Chris Maloney [14].

To alert us to why they have added the word intelligent to the title of their book, let me quote from their book:

As an adjective, kind means being a sympathetic, helpful or of a forbearing nature ,and importantly for our subject, being inclined to bring pleasure or relief. It is important to keep it rooted in its deeper meanings, though it can easily become a mere synonym for individual acts of generosity, sentiment and affection, for a general, fuzzy "kindliness". The Old English noun "cynd" metamorphosed through Middle English to be come "kinde" and into our modern language as "kind". The word meant "nature", "family", "lineage" – "kin". It indicated what we are, who we are and that we are linked together, in the present and across time. The word "kindness" indicates the quality or state of being kind. It describes a condition in which people recognise their nature, know and feel that this is essentially one with that of their kin, understand and feel their interdependence, feel responsibility for their successors and express all this in attitudes and actions towards each other. Kindness is both an obligation to one's kin born of our understanding of our connectedness, and the natural expression of our attitudes and feelings arising from this connectedness. It is closely linked with the concept of compassion (literally, suffering with), sympathy (fellow feeling) and the biblical word "agape" (neighbourly or "brotherly" love). People who are "rooted" in a sense of kinship with each other are inclined to attentiveness to the other, to gentleness, warmth and creativity on their behalf. Kindness is kinship felt and expressed.

Kindness involves the risk of getting things wrong, maybe of being hurt somehow in the process. Kindness is most effective when directed by intelligence. It really is no good fixing the boiler for the elderly lady next door if you are not qualified in gas engineering, however good she or you feel about your generosity. Knowing not to feed a hungry newborn with pasta can be a help. Understanding the challenges of adolescence can lead to more productive, and less exhausting parenting[14].

Compassion: Feelings Thoughts and Actions

Compassion can be defined as a family of responses (including one's own), which can, and does, include one or all of the following three responses:

Feelings: this may include: concern; sadness; love: empathy: anger; pity or none. If none you may respond by some of the following:

Thoughts: "How awful"; "Why do we let this happen?"; "I must do something about it". "Poor blighter". "Not my problem". "Serves them right". If none, you may then be driven to:

Action: Give money; raise money; help the individual write to the press; volunteer; go on a march or walk on the other side of the road and do nothing.

A feeling may precipitate a thought that may well lead to some action. It is also often the case that you may respond with action without feeling anything, and of course the opposite is true, you may have strong feelings but do nothing about it.

The most often quoted example of feeling and action without thought was when the concentration camps were liberated in the Second World War. Many soldiers on seeing the poor emaciated prisoners gave them their own emergency rations, which, in many instances, killed the starving prisoner. Ballatt and Campling's concept of *Intelligent Kindness* does not exclude feelings but ensures the action is guided by intelligence.

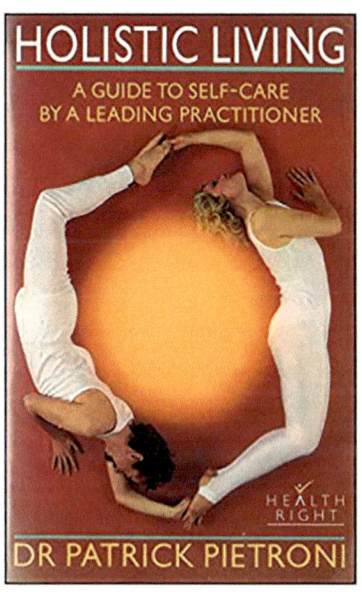

CULTIVATING COMPASSION

Self Compassion

In my book *Holistic Living* [15], a guide to self-care, I outline some of these key issues. By now they are very well publicised as a voluminous array of self-help activities. This list is large and below is a list for you to consider:

Breathing and relaxation exercises
Yoga, meditation, mindfulness
Physical exercise, walking, jogging, team sports
Reading poetry, listening to music
Retreating to your favourite place

Joining a group of like-minded people
Keeping a diary
Singing in a choir
Gardening
Learning a new skill, cooking, pottery
Adopting a pet – cat, dog, horse
Seeking a mentor or trusted friend or counsellor
Nearly forgot – taking care of your diet

There is no doubt however, that we are all able to cope with the challenges we face if we are supported by another human being who will "bear witness" and be there for us when we are suffering. If we can accept our own limitations and needs, we are far more likely to be compassionate to the suffering of others. The following poem has certainly helped me.

COMPASSION AND THE OTHER

It is in the safety of
my own quiet corner
that I can acknowledge
my own shadow

Filled as it is with
all the blocks and hurdles
that limit my capacity
for compassion
to the other.
My shadow is my own other.

Know it
befriend it
you will find it
possible
to approach all the others
you will meet
on your own
journey
with compassion.

Patrick Pietroni [16]

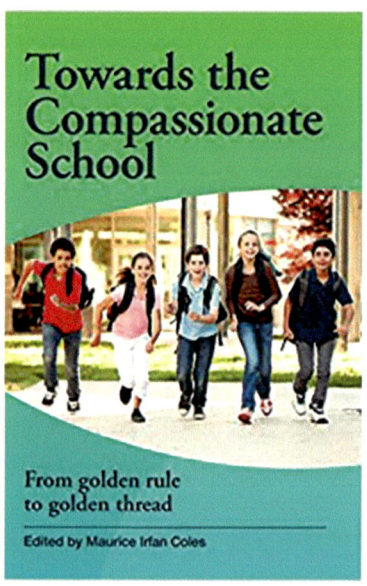

Within Educational Establishments

Maurice Irfan Coles edited a comprehensive book entitled *Towards the Compassionate School: from Golden Rule to Golden Thread*[17]. He summarised his life's work in the final chapter as follows:

A compassionate school would exhibit all or some of the following characteristics. It would:
- *have compassion as its key ongoing organizing principle, so that it permeates everything the school does*
- *ensure compassion infuses and enthuses its curriculum content and curricular processes*
- *ensure compassion forms the bedrock of initial teacher and continuing professional development*

- *have signed the Charter for Compassion with the Golden Rule as its heart, and with the Golden Thread pulsating through its arteries*
- *use the taxonomy of compassion 'acts for love', as a key vehicle for both values transmission and as an audit tool*
- *have a complete workforce, including school governors and managers, who articulate the vision and live its principles*
- *have leaders, staff, parents and carers who model these values*
- *have a pupil population that aspires to these ideals, which will be clearly visible, both in their behaviours and in how they treat each other and adults in the school and beyond*
- *employ pupil, staff and whole-system assessments that do not undermine good practice but build upon it*
- *enjoy a culture of listening based upon empathetic understanding and a willingness to appreciate the view of the other*
- *each pupils some knowledge of how the brain works so that they understand we are wired for compassion*
- *allow its pupils and staff the space to contemplate, to reflect, to be mindful*
- *be proactive in its local and wider community*
- *be proactive in building local, national and international cohesion*
- *be a health-promoting school that pays due regard to the social, emotional and spiritual aspect of learning*
- *be a school that really values educating the heart*
- *be a school that is culturally inclusive and meets the needs of its diverse pupil population*
- *be a school that safeguards its pupils and teaches them skills to live in this digital age*
- *practice restorative justice as part of its behaviour policy*
- *be a school that balances high attainment with self-esteem*
- *be a campaigning school, championing the rights of others*

and the needs of the planet
- *celebrate and regularly praise kindness and compassionate acts*
- *encourage the ideal of service, collegiality and love in action for our global interconnected universe*
- *be a happy school with lots of smiling faces.*

We can sum up the characteristics of the compassionate educator and the compassionate school as 'love in action'. The adoption of this principle in everything we do in school life provides the Golden Thread through which we help young people create a better and more just world. Students must still attain, must develop academic, vocational and social skills, but should have a more balanced purpose of elevating service, rather than self, as the key virtue. If pupils leave our care celebrating the maxim that 'universal compassion is the only guarantee of morality' (Schopenhauer, cited in Dossey, 2013:6), we will have gone some way to fulfilling our responsibilities to future generations.[17]

Within Health-Care Settings

The Royal College of Psychiatrists (UK) published a faculty report in 2015 entitled Compassion in care: ten things you can do to make a difference. [18] In the introduction they wrote:

> *The purpose of this faculty report is to highlight why compassion is important, what gets in the way of delivering compassionate care and what can be done to facilitate it. The intended audience is primarily psychiatrists, but the actions identified to encourage compassionate care can apply to all health and social care professionals in any care setting.*

I would also add that the following list could apply to many other work settings:

How to demonstrate compassion: ten things you can do every day

1. *Be alive to your internal world – your capacity to tolerate distress, your emotional state and your level of fatigue, and take measures to maintain resilience or improve matters if needed.*
2. *Support the development of systems at work that give you and your colleagues a space to reflect on what you are doing and attend those events when they happen.*
3. *Remember that patients are usually in distress – that is why they are in your care. Treat them as people, not diagnoses. Remember the importance of basic communication and interview skills: intelligent listening, mindfulness with regard to dynamics, proper interview setting.*
4. *Model compassionate behaviour for trainees and other members of staff. Like it or not, you work in a complex system, and how you are affects others around you.*
5. *If there is system problem, do not work around it or ignore it. Addressing it is your duty, and in the end it is better for you, your colleagues and your patients. Remember, the standard you walk by is the standard you accept.*

6. *If there is a problem with someone else's behaviour or attitude, challenge it appropriately. Although this is difficult, it is essential and again better for you, your colleagues and your patients.*

7. *Make sure training activities foster the right behaviour and values among trainees.*

8. *Respect systems, but think of people and relationships. It is people who get things done, not forms on a computer. Go see someone rather than call, call rather than email. Foster good working relationships. Make tea. And do the washing up.*

9. *Make the patient in front of you your primary concern, but balance actions for that patient with actions you and the organisation might have to take for others.*

10. *Pay attention and be respectful. When in consultations or meetings, turn phones and tablets off. Be in the situation, not somewhere else. And when your business is done, leave. Your time and energy are limited, and so are those of others.*

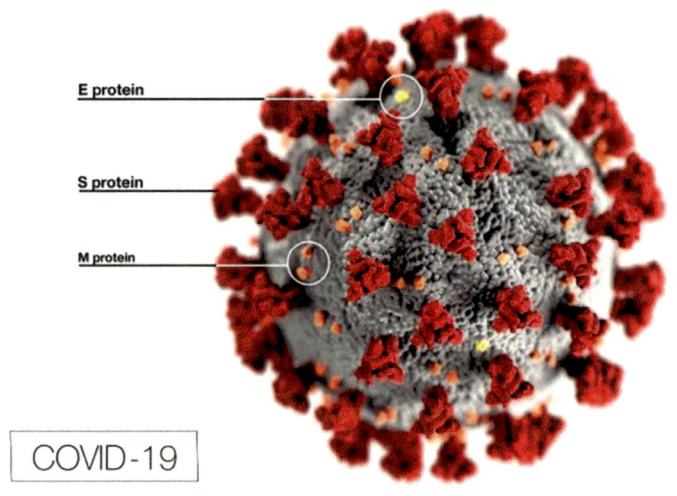

E protein

S protein

M protein

COVID-19

Global Compassion

Book Three of this series was dedicated to exploring what compassion for our environment required us to do. In 1970, Charles Reich wrote his book *The Greening of America* [19], writing during a period of American history when the peace movement drew fire from supporters of the Vietnam War and 'flower children' ran the gauntlet with the National Guard, it is perhaps understandable that his vision of Utopia should have reflected his sense of hope for the future more accurately than his ability to predict its outcome.

Now 50 years later we are living through the worst pandemic that any of us has witnessed. Covid-19 has brought havoc and death all over the planet Earth. Some experts have already suggested this world crisis as a "dress rehearsal' for what is to come as we face the consequences of climate change.

We have become increasingly aware that the consequences of this pandemic not only cause serious illness and many deaths, but can leave many who are not affected with much psychological suffering and mental health problems. The Greater Good Science Center at University of Berkeley [20] undertakes both research and training into how to cultivate compassion. Here are some of the research findings as to why we should practice compassion:

> *Scientific research into the measurable benefits of compassion is young. Preliminary findings suggest, however, that being compassionate can improve health, well-being, and relationships. Many scientists believe that compassion may even be vital to the survival of our species, and they're finding that its advantages can be increased through targeted exercises and practice. Here are some of the most exciting findings from this research so far.*

- *Compassion makes us feel good: Compassionate action (e.g., giving to charity) activates pleasure circuits in the brain, and compassion training programs, even very brief ones, strengthen brain circuits for pleasure and reward and lead to lasting increases in self-reported happiness.*

- *Being compassionate—tuning in to other people in a kind and loving manner—can reduce risk of heart disease by boosting the positive effects of the Vagus Nerve, which helps to slow our heart rate.*
- *One compassion training program has found that it makes people more resilient to stress; it lowers stress hormones in the blood and saliva and strengthens the immune response. Compassion training may also help us worry less and be more open to our negative emotions.*

- *Compassion could improve our mental health: One research review found that practicing compassion meditation improved participants' emotional life, positive thinking, relationships, and empathy.*
- *Brain scans during loving-kindness meditation, which directs compassion toward suffering, suggest that, on average, compassionate people's minds wander less about what has gone wrong in their lives, or might go wrong in the future; as a result, they're happier.*
- *Practicing compassion could make us more altruistic. In turn, it may also help us overcome empathic distress and become more resilient in the face of others' suffering.*
- *Compassion helps make caring parents: Brain scans show that when people experience compassion, their brains activate in neural systems known to support parental nurturance and other caregiving behaviors.*
- *Compassion helps make better spouses: Compassionate people are more optimistic and supportive when communicating with others.*
- *Compassion helps make better friends: Studies of college friendships show that when one friend sets the goal to support the other compassionately, both friends experience greater satisfaction and growth in the relationship.*
- *Compassion helps make better doctors: Medical students who train in compassion feel less depressed and lonely and avoid the typical declines in compassion that happen during medical school.*
- *Feeling compassion for one person makes us less vindictive toward others.*
- *Restraining feelings of compassion chips away at our commitment to moral principles.*
- *Employees who receive more compassion in their workplace*

see themselves, their co-workers, and their organization in a more positive light, report feeling more positive emotions like joy and contentment, and are more committed to their jobs. A compassionate workplace culture is linked to less burnout, greater teamwork, and higher job satisfaction.

- *More compassionate societies—those that take care of their most vulnerable members, assist other nations in need and have children who perform more acts of kindness—are the happier ones.*
- *Compassionate people are more socially adept, making them less vulnerable to loneliness; loneliness has been shown to cause stress and harm the immune system.* [20]

Conclusion

Professor Paul Gilbert at the University of Derby, UK has assembled much of the material outlined in this book and established the organisation, *The Compassionate Mind Foundation.* [21] His team is now the leading organisation in the UK and USA. The following table summarises our current understanding of what is labelled evolution informed psychotherapy in Compassion Focused Therapy (CFT).[22]

	DESCRIPTION	IMPLICATIONS

1. Human brain as an evolved organ	• Like all living beings we are part of the flow of life.
	• We have a human brain we did not design, but evolved through millions of years of evolution, which has inbuilt emotion and motivational systems.
		• Our evolved brains' primary motivations are to survive and reproduce.
		• Our brains have inbuilt motives and motive conflicts:
		  - Harm avoidance, food, sex, competitive, caring, status.
		• Motives organise our minds:
		  - Attention, thinking behaviour, imagery, emotion, sensory.

2. Brain capacities	• As a result of evolution, our brain has "trade-offs", constraints and many built-in biases.
	• Old Brain Functions are focused on survival and reproduction.
	• New Brain Functions, especially those supporting social intelligence (see Gilbert, Chapter 3, this volume), are focused on awareness and meta-awareness.
		• Old Brain Functions:
		  - Motives: harm avoidance, food, sex, caring, status.
		  - Emotions: anger, anxiety, sadness, joy.
		  - Behaviours: fight, flight, shutdown, courting, caring.
		• New Brain Functions and competencies:
		  - Language/symbols, self-monitoring/awareness, self-criticism, imagination, planning, rumination, worry, shame, integration.
		• We get caught in 'old brain—new brain' loops.
		  - We have the new capacity of thinking, but run on "old" psychological systems, whereby external 'threat' stimulus is brought inside our minds (e.g. imagination, rumination, worry, self-blame).

3. Brain/mind shaped by social contexts	• A genetic lottery for how our brains are built. • The environments in which we grow and the parenting we receive influence our genetic expression and our developing phenotypes. • Phenotypes are the expressed or manifest traits/outputs that are observable or measurable	• Born with a pre-determined set of genes we have inherited from parents. • Epigenetics and the process of methylation influences genetic expression. Stressful environments, in contrast to safe and predictable environments, turn genes on and off in different ways as the child is developing his/her phenotypes that prepare them for the environmental niche in which s/he is growing.

- As therapists, with the help of our clients, we aim to discover how our clients are primarily motivated to be in the world, and how that changes/shifts in different social contexts (e.g. work, family, friends, romantic partner).
  - For example: guided discovery, Socratic questioning.
- Over the course of therapy the therapist then focuses on exploring how particular motives impact and organise our minds.

- Psychodynamic and Jungian therapies focused on old-brain capacities (e.g. motives and archetypes, sex, aggression). Cognitive therapies focused on new-brain capacities (e.g. automatic thoughts, reasoning). As therapists we can focus on both, as in reality it is a two-way street, where we can attend to the interaction between old brain—new brain processing loops.
  - For example, this could be demonstrated with the analogy of the 'Zebra in the Savannah'. If the Zebra senses a predator it will run away for safety (better safe than sorry), then go back to eating. Put a human brain in the Zebra, despite being safe, thoughts will continue such as "supose I get caught tomorrow, dying would be terrifying". Thus, external threat stimulus taken into the mind, and continues physiologital threat response in the body, an 'old brain—new brain' loop.
- Therapists then focus on developing a case formulation of the client based on Evolutionary Functional Analysis (EFA, see Gilbert, 2014; Chapter 3, this volume).

- This permits a de-shaming for our clients as so much of what has happened to them is not of their choosing, and is not their fault.
  - For example, ask yourself, "Would you be the same person if you had been kidnapped as a three-day old baby and raised by the Mafia?"
- Focus of therapy becomes what version of ourselves have we become and in what contexts, and what versions of ourselves are possible that we wish to cultivate (e.g. compassionate self, angry self, anxious self, for more see Gilbert, 2010, 2014).

	DESCRIPTION	IMPLICATIONS
	(e.g. styles of language or attachment).	• We are socially shaped, from gene expressions to our sense of self and values.
4. Brain and biases	• We have biases that shape how we see the world.	• Biased learning (e.g. fear of snakes, electricity). • Self-focused (grasping and aversion). • Kin preferences (nepotism). • In-group preferences (tribalism). • Negativity (better safe than sorry).

5. Brain caring motivation	• Parental investment (care for offspring — supporting allies).
	• Distress Signal/Distress Response
	• Human mammals evolved for forming (and needing) attachment and social lives
		• Humans have few offspring, cared for many years. Parental care involves moving towards distress signals from young to soothe and calm (emotion regulation for child), and this forms attachments.
		• Attachment system:
		  - Proximity seeking — desire closeness.
		  - Secure base — source of security and guidance to explore.
		  - Safe haven — source of comfort and emotion regulation.
		  - Later in life, close friends and partners take on these roles and suffering can arise if they don't.

6. Brain and affect system	• The brain has emotion regulation systems that impact how we interface with the world and ourselves.	• Threat and self-protect system:
		  - Focus on protection and safety-seeking, it activates and inhibits.
		  - Emotions: anger, anxiety, disgust.
		• Drive and achievement system:
		  - Incentive/resource focused, wanting, pursuing, achieving, activating.
		  - Emotions: drive, excite vitality.
		• Affiliative/soothing system:
		  -Non-wantng, affiliative focused, safeness, kindness, soothing.
		  - Emotions: content, safe connected.

- These biases can lead to inner (mental anguish, such as self-criticism) and outer conflicts (interpersonal), which can lead humans to engage in great cruelty, bringing suffering to ourselves and to others (both mentally and physically).
- Therapists can explore with their clients how these biases were not 'chosen' by them, and how they operate in their daily life, which informs the ongoing EFA for the client, then how to counteract them with different forms of compassion focusing.
  - To indicate threat, therapists could provide clients the example of the 'Christmas Shopper'. The person who goes into 10 shops, in 9 of which he/she is greeted in a friendly and helpful manner, but in the 10th shop he/she is greeted by a rude and unhelpful shop assistant. When the Christmas Shopper gets home, what does he/she tell their partner about? The negative experience: an example of negativity bias.
- The therapist aims to create an internalised, secure base and safe haven for the client by activating the compassionate self as an organising process and focus for self-identity.
- Therapist also acts as a model for compassion to the client in therapy, and seeks to create a secure base and safe haven enabling clients the opportunities to explore difficult memories, situations, thoughts, emotions in a therapeutic context of safeness.
- Understanding how the cilent has developed safety behavioural strategies is crucially important at this stage, which also informs the EFA.
- Therapist makes the distinction between safety (threat focused/preventive) and safeness (open, explorative and growth focused) (see Gilbert, 2014).

- The therapist with the client explore how we can operate from various emotion systems, and how each system can impact how we view ourselves and interact with others.
  - Process of psycho-education, guided discovery, Socratic questioning.
- The information ascertained further informs ongoing EFA for client.
- The therapist with the help of the client, aims to develop a balance between these affect systems.

EDITED BY **PAUL GILBERT**

compassion

Conceptualisations, Research
and Use in Psychotherapy

References

1. Pietroni, P. (2020). *Feel, Think and Act*. Unpublished.
2. Darwin, C. (1871). *The Descent of Man, and Selection in Relation to Sex*. London. John Murray.
3. Darwin, C. *ibid*.
4. Higgins, R. (1978). *The Seventh Enemy; the Human Factor in the Global Cris*is. New York. McGraw-Hill.
5. Barks, C. (1995). *The Essential Rumi*. New York. Harper Collins.
6. Shakespeare, W. *As You Like It, Act II, Scene VII (All the world's a stage)*. Available at https://www.poetryfoundation.org/poems/56966/speech-all-the-worlds-a-stage (last accessed April 2020).
7. Amitav Radiance. (2014). *Dreams*. Available at https://hellopoetry.com/poem/872369/dreams/ (last accessed May 2020).
8. MS Lim. (2015). *The Shrink Series 2*. Available at https://hello poetry.com/poem/1468205/humourousfrivolous-poems-the-shrink-series-2 (last accessed May 2020).
9. Adams, M.A. (2014). *For Love of the Imagination: Interdisciplinary Applications of Jungian Psychoanalysis*. Hove. Routledge.
10. Discoveria. (2012). *Maslow's Hierarchy of Needs*. Available at https://allpoetry.com/poem/9501557-Maslows-Hierarchy-of-Needs-by-Discoveria (last accessed May 2020).
11. Sagan, C. (1978). The dragons of Eden: speculations on the evolution of human intelligence. New York. Random House.
12. Bruening, L. Available at https://innermammalinstitute.org/ (last accessed February 2020).
13. Ballatt, J. & Campling, P. (2011). *Intelligent Kindness: Reforming the Culture of Healthcare.* London. RCPsych Publications.
14. Ballatt, J., Campling, P. & Maloney, C. (2020. 2nd Ed. First published 2011). *Intelligent Kindness: Rehabilitating the Welfare State*. London. RCPsych Publications.
15. Pietroni, P. (1986). *Holistic Living*. London. Everyman.
16. Pietroni, P. (2019). *Compassion and the Other*. Unpublished.
17. Coles, M. I. (Ed.). (2015). *Towards the Compassionate School: from Golden Rule to Golden Thread*. London. UCL Institute of Education Press.

18. The Royal College of Psychiatrists. (2015). *Compassion in care: ten things you can do to make a difference.* Available at www.rcpsych.ac.uk/docs/default-source/members/faculties/general-adult-psychiatry/general-adult-fr-gap-02-compassionate-care.pdf?sfvrsn=e6852ee1_2 (last accessed May 2020).

19. Reich, C.A. (1970). *The Greening of America.* New York. Random House.

20. Greater Good. Berkeley Wellness. University of California. (2020). *What is Compassion.* Available at https://www.berkeleywellness.com/healthy-mind/mind-body/article/what-compassion (last accessed May 2020).

21. *The Compassionate Mind Foundation.* Available at https://www.compassionatemind.co.uk/ (last accessed June 2020).

22. Gilbert, P. (Ed.). (2005). *Compassion.* Abingdon. Routledge.

Photo Credits

Shutterstock, pg. 12
The Allegory of the Cave – Jan Saenredam, pg. 13
Sigmund Freud – Wikimedia Commons, pg. 17
Robin Hood, pg. 22
Ivan Pavlov, pg. 24
Pavlov's Dogs. Image available at www.amazon.com, pg. 25
Table – Hemispheres of the brain, pg. 29
Illustration of the hemispheres of the brain, pg. 30
Loretta Breuning – Happy Brain Chemicals. Image available at:
     https://innermammalinstitute.org/, pg. 32
Psychology Word Cloud, pg. 33
Intelligent Kindness. Image available at www.amazon.com, pg. 36
Holistic Living. Image available at www.amazon.com, pg. 39
Towards the Compassionate School. Image available at
     www.amazon.com, pg. 42
Royal College of Psychiatrists. Image available at https://www.rcpsych.ac.uk/
     about-us/library-and-archives/our-history/the-rcpsych, pg. 45
Covid-19 illustration – Alissa Eckert, U.S. Centers for Disease Control
     and Prevention (CDC) and Dan Higgins, pg. 48
Compassion. Image available at www.amazon.com, pg. 56

Publisher
SF Design, llc / Fresco Books
Albuquerque, New Mexico
frescobooks.com

ISBN: 978-1-934491-78-2